century
Bravado

ISLAND   global
          TALENT

Published By Century Books Limted,
Unit I, Upside Station Building,
Solsbro Road, Torquay, Devon, TQ2 6FD.
books@centurybooksltd.co.uk   Published 2011.

Under license from Bravado Merchandising.
All rights reserved.

©2011 Photography
Rob Cable, Cable image agency

www.thewantedmusic.com

CONTENTS

The WANTED

MEET THE BAND!

Welcome to the official 2012 annual of your favourite boy band – The Wanted!

This fun-filled book is packed with facts, quizzes and stories about the boys. They are having a blast and they want to share the fun with you!

Since The Wanted formed in 2009, they have taken the UK by storm. Their very first single shot to number one and stayed in the charts for eleven weeks! With a nationwide tour and their American launch, the boys are super busy. But they always have time to share the adventure with their fans.

The boys love finding out about their fans. Fill out this backstage pass – and don't forget to add your photo!

BACKSTAGE PASS

STICK A PICTURE OF YOURSELF IN HERE

FIRST NAME:
....

SURNAME:
....

DATE OF BIRTH:
....

AGE:
....

The WANTED

JAY

jay

Jay comes from a large family and never planned on being in a band. He discovered he was good at dancing by accident when he followed his mum along to a dance class when he was 13.

This answered the question as to what he would study in college, and he had a blast there. When he graduated he went to loads of dance auditions but when he didn't get any of those jobs he figured he'd try the one looking for 'male vocalists' - turns out he could sing!

Home town:	Newark-on-Trent! (Nottingham)
Nickname:	Bird
Star sign:	Leo
Favourite colour:	Red
Favourite animal:	Lizard
Favourite meal:	Quorn Savoury Eggs. It's a meal if you eat 12.
Musical heroes:	Cat Stevens, Newton Faulkner, Seth Lakeman, The Venga Boys.
Favourite book:	Wizards First Rule.
Favourite film:	Avatar.
Greatest fear:	Friends/family dying.
Biggest celebrity crush:	Mila Kunis
Most embarrassing moment:	Wetting myself twice in a row at primary school in the dinner hall.

Fun fact: Jay has a twin called Tom.

Jay likes to write and illustrate stories about the members of the band when he has some 'down-time'. Here is his own doodle story…

JAY'S RIDDLES

Next I have a series of The Wanted related riddles for you to figure out. They're pretty awesome

For real!

Is Jay your favourite boy in the band? Fill out this section to remind yourself of why he's so great!

Jay is my favourite because…

What would you do if you could hang out with Jay for a day?

Jay and I would be BFFs because…

My favourite lyric that Jay sings…

When we meet, I'll say…

And I'll wear…

9

The WANTED

MAX

Max didn't always want to be a singer. When he was growing up, he lived and breathed football. His greatest ambition was to become a professional player, and he was even signed up by Oldham Football Club. But fate had something else in store for this Manchester boy!

Max will always love football, and he hasn't lost touch with his friends from school. He's still the mischievous lad who kept getting sent out of class! But now he has found his dream, and he's having great fun making it come true.

Home town:	Manchester
Star sign:	Virgo
Favourite colour:	Black
Favourite animal:	Great White Shark
Favourite meal:	Full English
Musical heroes:	Elvis, Nat King Cole & M
Favourite book:	Jaws
Favourite film:	Jurassic Park & Jaws
Greatest fear:	Losing People
Biggest celebrity crush:	Michelle Keegan
Most embarrassing moment:	That Last Question

Fun fact: Max used to be in a band called Avenue, and together they reached the Bootcamp stage of The X Factor!

MAX'S RIDDLE

Rough Intro

Jay likes to write and illustrate stories about the members of the band when he has some 'down-time'. Here is his Max doodle story...

Max looked through the dirty window at our house and sighed. He'd had enough, finally he reached and opened the window high up on the 20th floor and jumped right through it. Outside, it was a sheer drop for the entire 20 floors, and there was nothing but concrete at the bottom. He was completely unhurt.

How did Max survive?

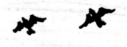

Max had had enough of window cleaning, he opened the window & jumped inside!

Is Max your favourite boy in the band? Fill out this section to remind yourself of why he's so great!

Max is my favourite because...

What would you do if you could hang out with Max for a day?

Max and I would be BFFs because...

My favourite lyric Max sings...

When we meet, I'll say...

And I'll wear...

11

The WANTED

SIVA

Siva loves playing the guitar and is always in his home studio when he has time off. From the time he was a kid, he has written and performed his own music. He spent time modelling and doing a bit of acting, but music was always his first love.

Siva keeps diaries and loves reading, this helps him when it comes to making up lyrics. He knows the best songs come from the heart!

Home town:	Dublin
Nickname:	Seev
Star sign:	Scorpio
Favourite colour:	Blue
Favourite animal:	Red Panda
Favourite meal:	Shepards Pie
Musical heroes:	Michael Jackson
Favourite book:	Dan Brown Digital Fortress
Favourite film:	Bicentennial man
Greatest fear:	Pokka Dots
Biggest celebrity crush:	Jessica Alba
Most embarrassing moment:	Trousers falling down on stage at the Arqiva Awards

Fun fact: Siva comes from a big family – six boys and two girls!

Rough Intro

Jay likes to write and illustrate stories about the members of the band when he has some 'down-time'. Here is his Siva doodle story...

Siva was found bruised, bloody, and unconscious in our flat. Big Kev is trying to work out who did it, before Sunday ends. Nathan said he was sleeping after his dinner.
Tom said he was cooking for everyone.
Jay said he was cleaning up Lizard crap.
Max said he was playing Championship manager.
And Jayne said she was collecting our mail.

Who battered Siva to a pulp?

It was Jayne.

There's no mail on Sunday!

13

TOM

Tom is never happy sitting still for long. He loves sport, but he knew from the moment he first picked up a guitar that music was what he wanted to do.

In pursuit of his dream, Tom started singing in the pubs and clubs around Bolton. He developed his writing skills, and got as much experience as he could. Tom has never wanted to do anything else besides music so has worked very hard to make his dream come true.

Home town:	Bolton
Nickname:	Roy
Star sign:	Leo
Favourite colour:	Blue
Favourite animal:	Parrot
Favourite meal:	Indian
Musical heroes:	Nirvana & Oasis
Favourite book:	Crime books
Favourite film:	The Butterfly Effect
Greatest fear:	Heights
Biggest celebrity crush:	Mila Kunis
Most embarrassing moment:	Went on a first date and fell down a grid

Fun fact: Tom was in a Take That tribute band called Take That II.

TOM'S RIDDLE

Rough Intro

Jay likes to write and illustrate stories about the members of the band when he has some 'down-time'. Here is his Tom doodle story...

When Tom was on the set of our video for "Lightning, he took a small stroll into the desert. There, he was kidnapped by a group of angry and hungry Ghetto-Goblins. They gave him the chance to say his last words, which would determine how they killed him.

If he told a lie, they would beat box him to death. If he told the truth, they'd break dance him to death.

What did he say to escape?

He said "You will beat box me to death".
... Get it?

Is Tom your favourite boy in the band? Fill out this section to remind yourself of why he's so great!

Tom is my favourite because...

What would you do if you could hang out with Tom for a day?

Tom and I would be BFFs because...

My favourite lyric Tom sings...

When we meet, I'll say...

And I'll wear...

15

The WANTED

NATHAN

Nathan grew up surrounded by music from the start. His whole family is musical and Nathan began writing songs when was very young, and he has always loved singing. It's taken a lot of hard work to get to be in the band and he loves performing in front of the fans, especially when they sing along. If he wasn't in a band, he's not sure what he would be doing!

Home town:	Gloucester
Nickname:	Nath
Star sign:	Aries
Favourite colour:	Red
Favourite animal:	Monkey
Favourite meal:	Spag Bol
Musical heroes:	Stevie Wonder, Boyz II Men, Michael Buble, Jamie Cullum, John Legend
Favourite book:	Ain't read a book in ages but used to love Darren Shan books
Favourite film:	Taken
Greatest fear:	Exposed heights
Biggest celebrity crush:	Rosie Huntington Whitely
Most embarrassing moment:	Not really had a stand out embarrassing moment but usually have them on a daily basis!

Fun fact: Nathan is the baby of the band!

NATHANS RIDDLE

Nathan has just moved in to a 12th story flat. Every day we wait in the car as he takes the elevator down to us. When he gets home, he goes up to the 6th floor then walks to the 12th. <u>But</u> on rainy days he goes up with the elevator to the 12th floor where he lives.

Why does Nath do that?

Nathan is a midget.

He can only reach the 6th floor button.

But when it rains he uses his umbrella to push it!

Is Nathan your favourite boy in the band? Fill out this section to remind yourself of why he's so great!

Nathan is my favourite because…

What would you do if you could hang out with Nathan for a day?

Nathan and I would be BFFs because…

My favourite lyric Nathan sings…

When we meet, I'll say…

And I'll wear…

The Journey to Stardom

So how did it all begin, and what brought together these five extraordinary lads?

In 2009, some of the biggest names in the music business decided to create a brand-new boy band. They wanted to find some of the best talent the country had to offer, and give them the chance to make their dreams come true. Hundreds of lads saw the same advert – 'Wanted: Male Vocalists'. And from across the UK, five future stars began an unforgettable journey.

ax knew what he didn't want to do – it was
juring out what he did want to do that was
e problem! He had turned his back on a
omising football career and now he wasn't
re which way to turn. He eventually decided
pursue a music career with the band
venue, but his hopes of appearing on The
Factor were dashed when it was revealed
at Avenue already had a manager. Then,
st when it seemed as though his dream of a
areer in music was over, he got the break he

had been waiting for. He was asked to be part
of a brand-new band!

Nathan was at stage school. To earn money
in his spare time, he found work through the
agency that was attached to the school.
Then, one day, the agency sent him along to
an audition for a new boy band – along with
every other boy in his year!

Meanwhile, Tom had been trying to progress as a singer. He was living in Sheffield and performing in local bars and clubs, but he was still looking for his big break. Then a casting company called him to ask if he would like to audition for a band.

Jay was looking for work after his final year of college when a chance internet search led him to the advert for male vocalists. He was longing to find a job after his years of studying, so he jumped at the chance to audition.

Siva was working in London as a model at the time. He had always loved playing music – the song he wrote for his graduation ceremony had people in tears! But it wasn't until his brother Trevor told him about the advert that he really focused on making music his career.

The auditions were tough. The boys were tested in every aspect of performance, including dance, singing to camera and song choice. The demanding boot camp stage pushed them to their limits.

20

Of course, chemistry was vital – the band had to blend together well. A lot of time was spent checking different combinations of singers. Even when it seemed as if the final five had been chosen, there was a last-minute check with seven new boys being tried out. But at long last, after their nerves had been totally wrung out, Max, Tom, Jay, Nathan and Siva were told the good news. They were in the band!

Turn to page 32 to find out what happened next!

QUIZ Part 1

GENERAL KNOWLEDGE

How much do you really know about The Wanted? Start this super-quiz challenge and find out if you're their number-one supporter or just a fair-weather fan!

Answer the questions below and write down your score. There are five sections to the quiz, and in the final part you will find out whether you know everything about The Wanted!

1. Who is the eldest member of The Wanted?

2. What was The Wanted's first single?

3. What was the name of the band that Max was in before The Wanted??

4. What is the name of The Wanted's record label?

5. What was the name of the single that The Wanted released for Comic Relief?

6 .Is it true that The Wanted shared a house when they first got together?

7. Which member of The Wanted was once signed up by a football club?

8. Two of The Wanted boys have twins – but which ones?

9. Where did Nathan grow up?

10. Who used to sneak into his brother's room and play his guitar?

The WANTED

DISCOGRAPHY

The WANTED
Release date: 25th October 2010

1. All Time Low
2. Heart Vacancy
3. Lose My Mind
4. Replace Your Heart
5. Hi & Low
6. Let's Get Ugly
7. Say It On The Radio
8. Golden
9. Weakness
10. Personal Soldier
11. Behind Bars
12. Made
13. A Good Day For Love To Die

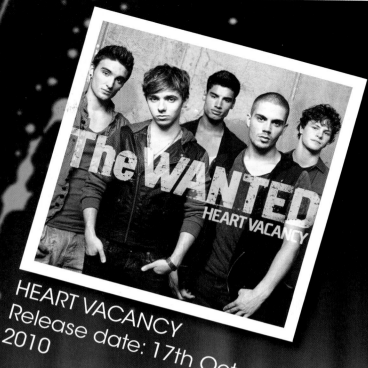

ALL TIME LOW
Release date: 25th July
2010

HEART VACANCY
Release date: 17th October
2010

LOSE MY MIND
Release date: 26th December
2010

GOLD FOREVER
Release date: 13th March
2011

GLAD YOU CAME
Release date: 10th July
2011

The WANTED
LYRICS

The WANTED
ALL TIME LOW

ALL TIME LOW

___ won't do it
___ won't do it
___ won't do it
Fighting won't knock you out
Of my ___

Hiding won't hide it
___ won't hide it
Like I ain't tried it
Everyone's tried it now
And failed ___

So when you gonna let me
When you gonna let me ___
___

And if you know
How do you get ___ from a ___
___ ___
I'm in ___
Seems like ___ is
The only thing I'll never know
How do you get out
Get out

'Cos ___ won't do it
___ won't do it
___ won't do it
___ won't drown it out
___ ___ ___

When I'm standing on the ___
___
Waiting at the ___
Or I'm late for ___
A vital ___
If you call me now girl
Without ___
I would try to ___ ___

But if you know
How do you get ___ from a
___ ___ ___
I'm in ___
It seems like ___ is

The only thing I never know
How do you get ___ from an
___ ___ ___

I can't even find a place to ___
How do I choose between my
___ and ___
'Til it ceases I never know
How do you get ___ from a ___
___ ___

A ___ a ___ a ___ a
A ___ a ___ a ___
Can you ___ ___
A ___ a ___ a ___ a
A ___ a ___ a ___
Can't you ___ ___
A ___ a ___ a ___ a
A ___ a ___ a ___
Can you ___ ___
A ___ a ___ a ___ a
A ___ a ___ a ___

And if you know
How do you get ___ from a
___ ___ ___
I'm in ___
It seems like ___ is
The only thing I never know
How do you get ___ from an
___ ___ ___
I can't even find a place to ___
How do I choose between my
___ and ___
'Til it ceases I never know
How do you get ___ from a ___
___ ___

I can't even find a place to ___
How do I choose between my
___ and ___
'Til it ceases I never know
How do you get ___ from a ___
___ ___

MAX

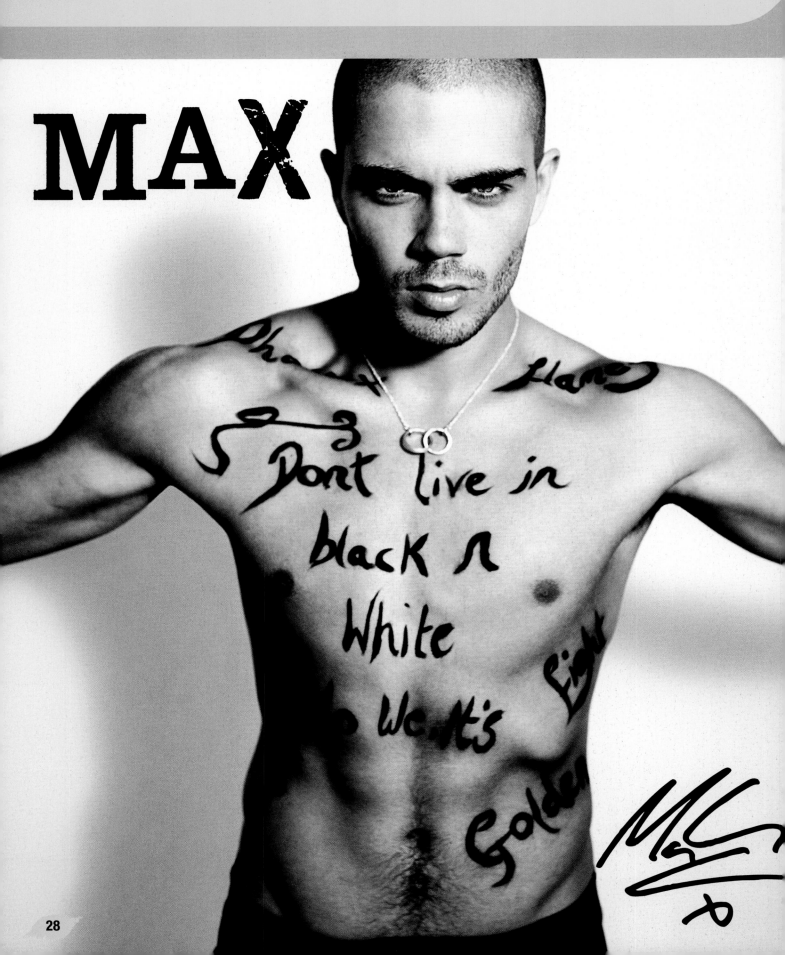

What's the best thing that's happened to you since forming The Wanted?
V Festival.

What did you like best about school?
4 o'clock....it finished.

What's your idea of the perfect date?
A zoo, then the pub.

How do you cope with the busy life of being in a band?
Make sure I always make my own down time somehow.

Do you have any pets?
4 dogs & 2 lizards.

What do you hope your life is like in ten years?
Married, kids, nice house, box at city & watching a movie directed by my brother Jack.

What was your favourite TV show when you were young?
Only fools and horses.

What's your favourite sport?
Football.

What's your favourite thing about yourself?
My jokes.

What makes you laugh?
My jokes.

When did you last cry and why?
I watched Ghost in the west end last week, hilarious, but i did sob a bit at the end.

If you weren't in The Wanted, what do you think you would be doing?
Working with my Dad, wheeling and dealing.

Do you prefer singing live or recording in a studio?
Live!!!

What's your earliest memory?
When my brother Jack fell and had a nail go through his lip... i was 3.

How would you like to be remembered?
Someone who made people happy

Who would like to sing a duet with?
Elvis...but alive....Lawson (my mate's band)

Are you a city lad or a country boy at heart?
City City City.

Are you a fashion fanatic?
No.

Are you allergic to anything?
Bad fashion....joke.

What's your most annoying habit?
My jokes.

Do you have any superstitions?
No.

How do you keep fit?
Eat sleep and wake up.

What's your favourite The Wanted lyric and why?
Glad You Came....isnt it obvious?

Do you believe in love at first sight?
I do now!

Do you do your own shopping?
Sometimes, I'm not a sultan i'm just in a pop band

What's your favourite place in the UK?
Manchester

What do you do to relax?
Go back to Manc and see my girl and my dogs

0061097
MAX GEORGE
LAS VEGAS POLICE DEPT

The Journey to Stardom..._{Part}

It was a weird time for the boys after they were told that they had made it into the band. They had to wait for two weeks before anything happened, and nobody else could be told about the band! Luckily they had each other, and their growing bond really strengthened in those early days.

As the boys learned more about the life that lay ahead of them, they had to keep pinching themselves to believe that it was real. They would be living the life of superstars and working with legendary songwriters such as Guy Chambers. The Wanted recorded their first tracks in January 2010 and soon felt as if they had known each other all their lives...

From the start, it was really important to the boys that they were involved in the creation of their own music and image. The Wanted are a new generation of boy band. They play their own instruments, write their own songs and definitely don't sit in a row on stools!

They all have very different personalities, but they have bonded better than they could have imagined, helped by the fact that they were housemates as well as bandmates! They share a ton of in-jokes, and feel amazingly lucky to be working with their best friends.

The Wanted went on a schools tour in the spring of 2010, feeling nervous but eager to share their music with the UK. The kids loved every single gig, screaming with excitement when the boys started to sing. Everyone was dancing and singing along with them, and the buzz was sensational. Now each of them knew for certain that this was their dream career. The schools tour wasn't about making money – it was about making fans. Everywhere they went, The Wanted gained loyal followers who would stick by them through thick and thin.

The next landmark moment was in summer 2010 when the boys got the chance to perform at Wembley for the Capital Summertime Ball. In just a few short months, they had gone

om auditioning in small rooms to
erforming in front of 70,000 people. It
l seemed so unreal! When their debut
ngle came out, the boys' hard work
ally started to pay off. Amid a week of
gnings, performances and interviews,
ll Time Low' headed straight for the
umber-one spot.

e Wanted had arrived!

HEART VACANCY

The WANTED
HEART VACANCY

Wooohh ohhhhh
I hear your ___ cry for ___
But you won't let me make it right
You were ___ but I decided that
you were worth the ___
Every night, you ___ ___ you
won't let me come inside
But the look in your eyes says I
can turn ___ ___

In your ___, in your ___, in your
___
I can tell you could fit one more
In your ___, in your ___, in your
___
I don't care who was there before

I hear your ___ cry for ___
Then you act like there's no room
Room for me or anyone, 'Don't Dis-
turb' is all I see
You closed the ___, turned the
___
On everything that we could ___
If ___ would move out, I'd fill the
vacancy

In your ___, in your ___, in your
___,
In your ___, in your ___, in your
___,

This ain't the ___ Hotel
Even though I know it well
Those ___ ___ they sure tell
In the way you hold yourself

Don't you ___, should you get
Another ___
Give me a chance
I'll make a ___ ___

In your ___, in your ___, in your
___

I can tell you could fit one more
In your ___, in your ___, in your
___
I don't care who was there before

I hear your ___ cry for ___
Then you act like there's no room
Room for me or anyone, 'Don't Dis-
turb' is all I see
You closed the ___, turned the
___
On everything that we could ___
If ___ would move out, I'd fill the
vacancy

In your ___, in your ___, in your
___
In your ___, in your ___, in your
___

When I ___ ___ you on the ___
and listen close

I hear your ___ cry for ___
Then you act like there's no room
Room for me or anyone,
'Don't Disturb' is all I see
You closed the ___, turned the
___
On everything that we could ___
If ___ would move out, I'd fill the
vacancy

In your ___, in your ___, in your
___
In your ___, in your ___, in your
___

GETTING TO KNOW...

JAY

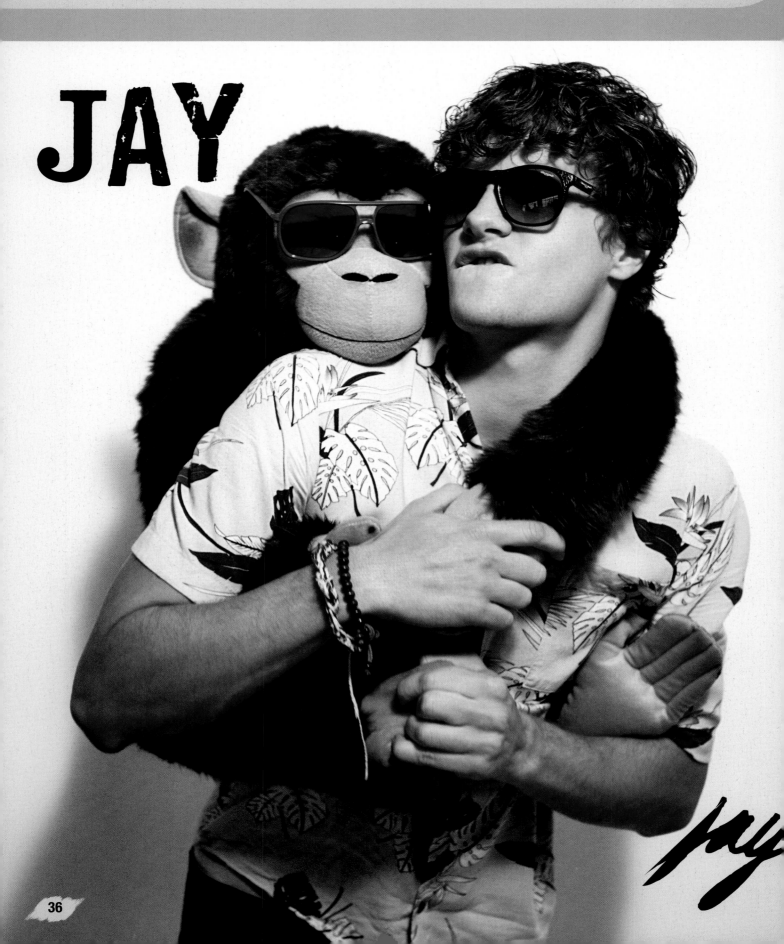

What's the best thing that's happened to you since forming The Wanted?
I met the other lads!

What did you like best about school?
My mates, and the teachers that made you feel adult when you were about 12.

What's your idea of the perfect date?
As long as she doesn't end up crying or slapping you it's gone pretty darn well. That and taking her home.

How do you cope with the busy life of being in a band?
Chill, in a pub, and act like a normal 21 year old.

Do you have any pets?
Yep, Neytiri or "Tia" my monitor lizard.

What do you hope your life is like in ten years?
Completely eco-freindly, and crazily amazing.

What was your favourite TV show when you were young?
Xena Warrior Princess or Blind Date.

What's your favourite sport?
Page turning.

What's your favourite thing about yourself?
How quick I can down a pint..

What makes you laugh?
Comedy.

When did you last cry and why?
Someone passing away.

If you weren't in The Wanted, what do you think you would be doing?
Bumming around wasting my "potential" as they say.

Do you prefer singing live or recording in a studio?
Singing live all the way.

What's your earliest memory?
Either kicking a football over the hedge into a lorry park, or putting my tongue in Mrs Duckmanton's mouth in nursery school, whichever was earlier...

How would you like to be remembered?
With fear and disgust.

Who would like to sing a duet with?
My Grandad.

Are you a city lad or a country boy at heart?
Townie. Not as in the posy chav term, someone who lives in a town.

Are you a fashion fanatic?
Ha ha ha ha ha!

Are you allergic to anything?
Nope.

What's your most annoying habit?
Saying "Yeah?" just after someone's said something.

Do you have any superstitions?
If someone speaks out loud about something they want to happen I touch wood that it does.

How do you keep fit?
Jumping on the spot like a five year old in gigs, or pint lifting for those massive guns.

What's your favourite The Wanted lyric and why?
"And we try, and we fall, and we live another day, and we rise, like a phoenix from the flames, and it "burns", but it turns out Golden". It sums up life a lot, it reminds you that you almost have no choice but to carry on. And the metaphor for the phoenix is slick as hell how it extends into the "burns" lyric, and THEN the word burns rolls perfectly into the tag line "It turns out Golden". Which we wrote with Jamie Hartman.

Do you believe in love at first sight?
I don't think so.

Do you do your own shopping?
Ha ha ha mostly! But I get help when I'm away and the Lizard needs a bit of love!.

What's your favourite place in the UK?
My hometown.

What do you do to relax?
Lizard watch, sit in a pub for hours, read, edit camera footage, love, watch come dine with me, or sing.

0061094
JAY McGUINESS
LAS VEGAS POLICE DE[

Trivia
DID YOU KNOW...?

- The Wanted performed at the Capital Summertime Ball at Wembley Stadium.

- Tom has hazel eyes.

- Jay's full name is James.

- Nathan supports Manchester United.

- Tom supports Bolton Wanderers

- Jay is a skilled tap dancer.

- Siva would love to travel in space!

- Max is hooked on The X Factor.

- Nathan once kissed Britney Spears.

- Jay loves pizza and cheese sandwiches.

QUIZ
Part 2

LYRICS CHALLENGE

A true fan of The Wanted knows every word to every song! Do you dare to test how good you really are? Complete each of these lines.

'Seen the change watching it...'

'When I'm standing on the yellow...'

'Fill my head with white...'

'You get bored and I get cold...'

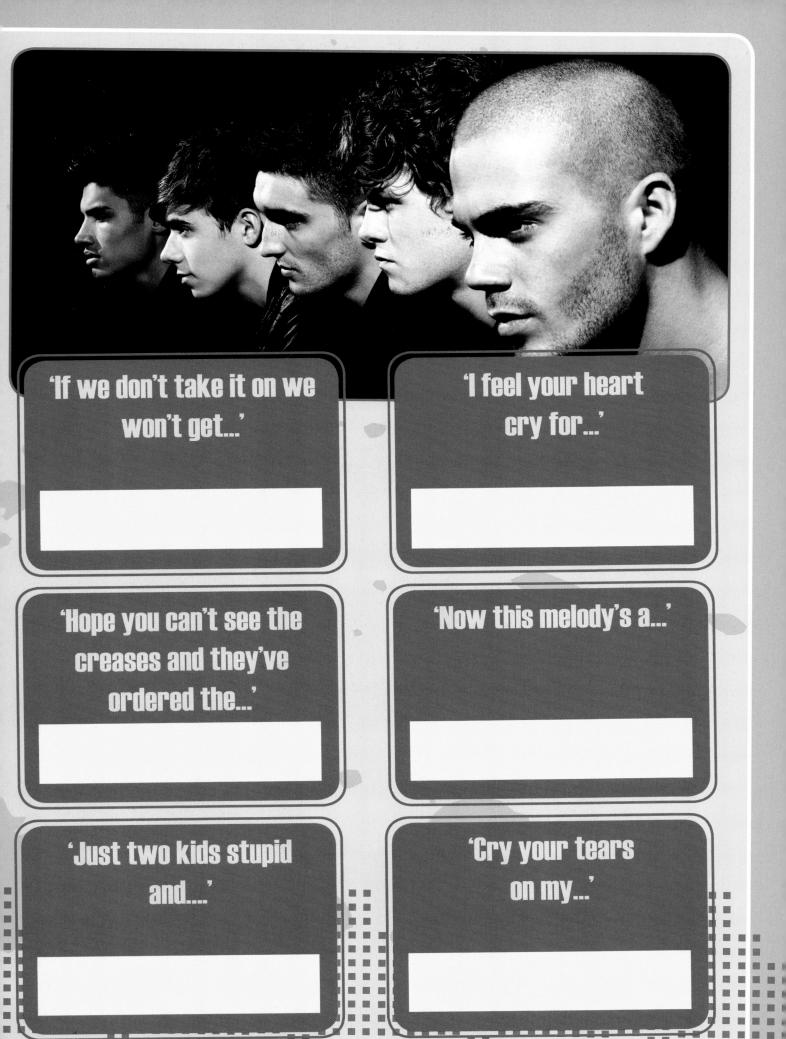

'If we don't take it on we won't get...'

'I feel your heart cry for...'

'Hope you can't see the creases and they've ordered the...'

'Now this melody's a...'

'Just two kids stupid and....'

'Cry your tears on my...'

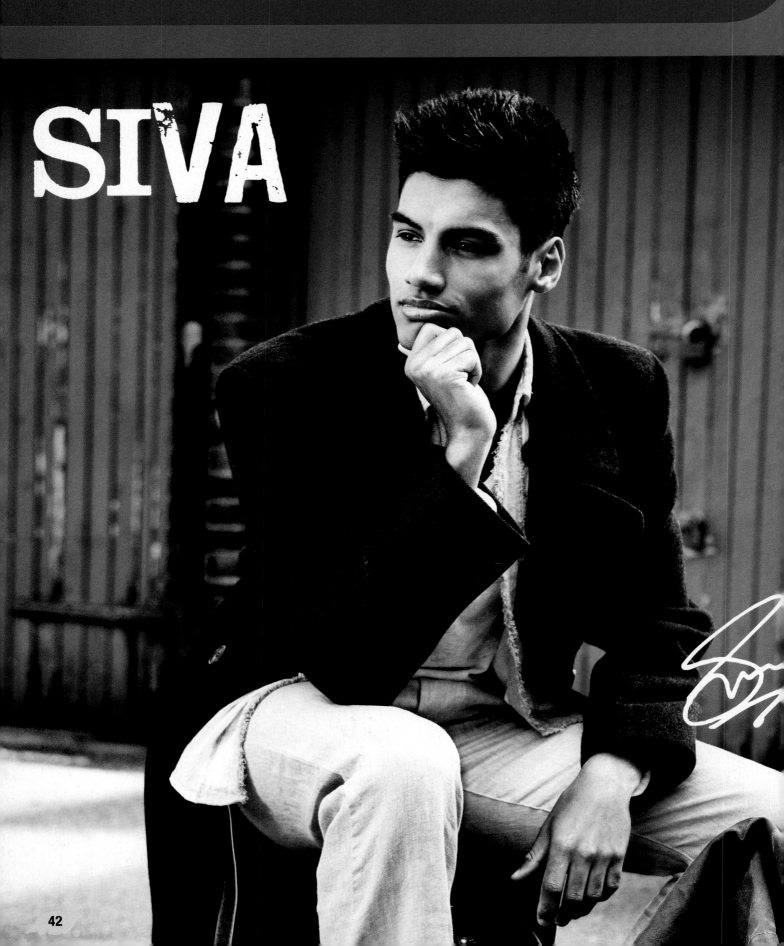

GETTING TO KNOW...

SIVA

42

What's the best thing that's happened to you since forming The Wanted?
Getting to release the Comic Relief single and raising so much money for the kids.

What did you like best about school?
The bus journey home from school, we used to get into a lot of mischief.

Who was your first love?
My beautiful Baba.

What's your idea of the perfect date?
An unforgetable one.

How do you cope with the busy life of being in a band?
Take my laptop everywhere to stay in contact with friends and family. And lots of chocolate :)

Do you have any pets?
Yeah a pet sloth called Nathan :)

What do you hope your life is like in ten years?
"I wanna be a millionaire so frickin bad".

What was your favourite TV show when you were young?
Transformers... "Robots in Disguise".

What's your favourite sport?
Rugby.

Do you ever obsess about your looks?
Haha only the hair, which i'm sure you will understand.

What's your favourite thing about yourself?
Good old Irish Charm.

What makes you laugh?
Billy Connelly.

When did you last cry and why?
When me and Nathan watched Marley and Me. he shed a tear too... because we are manly like that.

Do you think you would make a good boyfriend?
I'm a good listener and have big lips so yes!!

If you weren't in The Wanted, what do you think you would be doing?
I would be a superhero... failing that i would probably still be model.

Do you prefer singing live or recording in a studio?
Live of course!, Nothing better than the buzz from the crowd.

What's your earliest memory?
I remember holding my twins hand on our 3rd birthday party dancing away.

How would you like to be remembered?
I would like to not be remembered as "Siva the Diva" because i don't want that3 on my grave stone.

Who would like to sing a duet with?
Rihanna.

Are you a city lad or a country boy at heart?
Country boy, nothing better than going back home to the country side where mam lives.

Are you a fashion fanatic?
Fanatic no, but i do like to look good.

Are you allergic to anything?
Polka Dots.

What's your most annoying habit?
I mumble a lot.

How do you keep fit?
Everyday i do a workout and eat healthy when not on the road.

What's your favourite The Wanted lyric and why?
"Some days stay Gold Forever".

Do you believe in love at first sight?
Yes.

Do you do your own shopping?
Online yes.

What's your favourite place in the UK?
London! It's my new home since leaving Ireland.

What do you do to relax?
Light my candles (don't judge me!).

0061095
SIVA KANESWARAN

LAS VEGAS POLICE DEPT.

The WANTED
WORDSEARCH

N	S	D	N	E	I	R	F	A	N	S
I	N	R	S	G	E	A	V	F	S	O
S	O	G	A	A	A	I	S	W	N	N
O	I	D	U	T	S	C	E	M	A	F
G	T	N	T	S	I	M	M	S	T	S
A	I	V	G	R	B	U	R	E	H	E
J	D	N	Y	L	S	B	G	C	A	C
U	U	L	S	I	E	L	T	T	N	M
J	A	Y	C	W	S	A	T	O	U	R
U	R	E	S	M	A	X	T	A	M	Y
W	E	M	B	L	E	Y	N	J	I	B

There are twenty words hidden in this giant grid – can you find

Album	**Guitars**	**Si**
Auditions	**Jay**	**Sto**
Fame	**Lyrics**	**Stu**
Fans	**Max**	**To**
Friends	**Music**	**To**
Gigs	**Nathan**	**Wen**
	Single	

The WANTED
CROSSWORD

Use your insider knowledge of The Wanted to solve the clues and complete the crossword. Set a timer to see how fast you are!

DOWN
1. The youngest member of the band.
2. The band's first single.
3. The band member who has hazel eyes.
7. What colour eyes does Jay have?
9. The band member who grew up in Ireland.
10. What is Siva's favourite animal?
11. The band member who has a twin called Tom.

ACROSS
4. The first type of dance that Jay learned.
5. What is Tom' star sign?
6. The name of the 2011 tour..
8. Nathan's favourite football team.
11. The month that the band's first single was released.
12. The only Virgo in the band.

THE IBIZA TRIP

Grab your towel and your bikini – it's holiday time and the guys are taking you to Ibiza with them!

The video for 'Glad You Came' was shot in Ibiza, and these behind-the-scenes snaps show that The Wanted had a blast. It's a hard job but someone has to do it!

Cameras filmed everything
while The Wanted had fun
messing around . . .

. . . posing . . .

. . . playing games . . .

. . . and . . . er . . . paddling!

'Glad You Came' has a club feel that gets every listener in the mood for a party. And The Wanted know how to party!

The spirit of summer inspired the guys to daring feats . . .

. . . or were they just showing off for the models in the vid?

49

The vid was shot over the course of two days on two cameras, with an international crew behind the scenes.

The Wanted loved their new song, and they were hoping that it would bag them another number one. It was one of their favourite tracks from the new album, and they couldn't wait to see what their fans would think.

After all their hard work, they had earned a rest!

The WANTED
LOSE MY MIND

LOSE MY MIND

Oh, oh
Oh, oh

They say that ▓▓▓
▓▓▓ everything
But they don't know ▓▓▓
And the ▓▓▓ ▓▓▓ bring

Oh, oh
Oh, oh

'Cos you left a jagged ▓▓▓
And I can't ▓▓▓ it anymore

If ▓▓▓ was a physical pain
I could ▓▓▓ it, I could ▓▓▓ it
But you're hurting me from inside
of my ▓▓▓
I can't take it, I can't take it

I'm gonna ▓▓▓ my ▓▓▓
Oh, oh
I'm gonna ▓▓▓ my ▓▓▓
Oh, oh

I'd erase my ▓▓▓
If only I knew how

Fill my head with ▓▓▓ noise
If it would drown ▓▓▓ out
Kill the ▓▓▓

If ▓▓▓ was a physical pain
I could ▓▓▓ it, I could ▓▓▓ it
But you're hurting me from inside
of my ▓▓▓
I can't take it, I can't take it

I'm gonna lose my mind
Oh, oh

I'm gonna lose my mind
Oh, oh

And I'd rather be ▓▓▓
I'd rather go ▓▓▓
Than having you ▓▓▓ my every
thought
Then having you here inside my
▓▓▓

If ▓▓▓ was a physical pain
I could ▓▓▓ it, I could ▓▓▓ it
But you're hurting me from inside
of my ▓▓▓
I can't take it, I can't take it

I'm gonna ▓▓▓ my ▓▓▓
Oh, oh
I'm gonna ▓▓▓ my ▓▓▓
Oh, oh

Oh, oh
Oh, oh

GETTING TO KNOW...

TOM

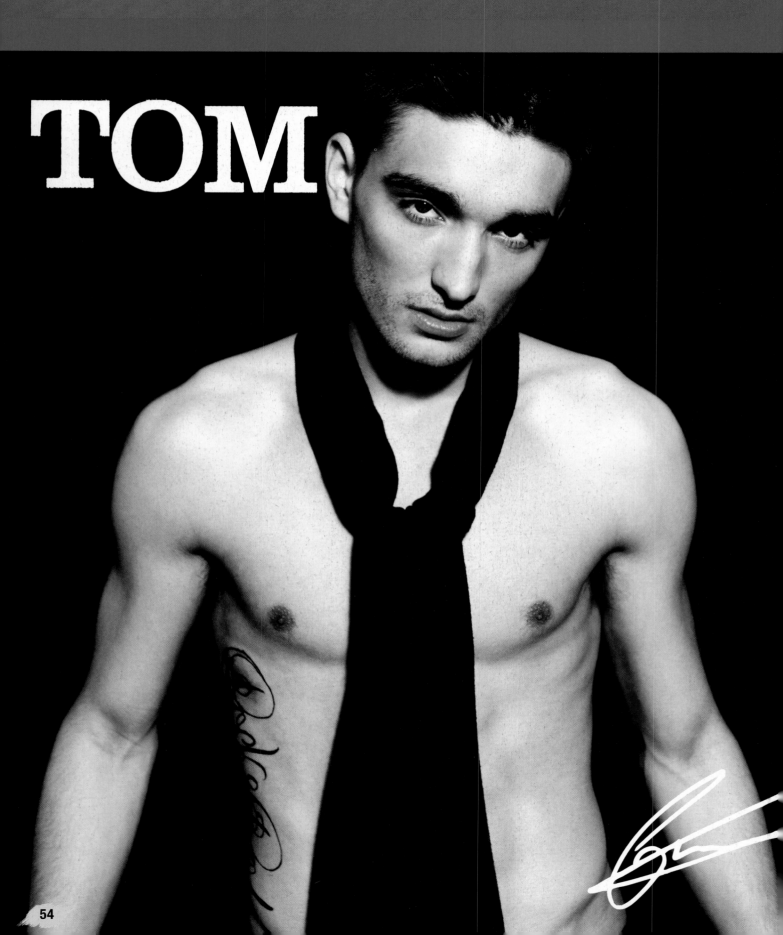

What's the best thing that's happened to you since forming The Wanted?
Travelling the world and performing on stage at Wembley.

What did you like best about school?
Physics.

What's your idea of the perfect date?
Pizza Express.

How do you cope with the busy life of being in a band?
I like to make free time to do normal things like drink beer and chill with friends.

Do you have any pets?
No pets.

What do you hope your life is like in ten years?
I hope to have a chain of properties and still be writing music and The Wanted are still around.

What was your favourite TV show when you were young?
CD:UK.

What's your favourite sport?
Football.

What's your favourite thing about yourself?
My personality.

What makes you laugh?
Cheap jokes make me laugh.

When did you last cry and why?
I last cried when I went to a penthouse in London and it was incredible (I'd had a few to drink).

If you weren't in The Wanted, what do you think you would be doing?
Working in something geographical.

Do you prefer singing live or recording in a studio?
Live.

What's your earliest memory?
My 5th football party.

How would you like to be remembered?
A happy, lively person.

Who would like to sing a duet with?
A duet with Liam Gallagher.

Are you a city lad or a country boy at heart?
City lad.

Are you a fashion fanatic?
No (I'm a scruffy bugger).

Are you allergic to anything?
No.

What's your most annoying habit?
Not cleaning up.

Do you have any superstitions?
Not walking under street signs.

How do you keep fit?
I don't keep fit (lazy).

What's your favourite The Wanted lyric and why?
Some days stay Gold Forever - because it's true.

Do you believe in love at first sight?
Yes.

Do you do your own shopping?
Yes I do my own shopping.

What's your favourite place in the UK?
London!

What do you do to relax?
Watch Jeremy Kyle and play guitar.

0061093
TOM PARKER
LAS VEGAS POLICE DEPT.

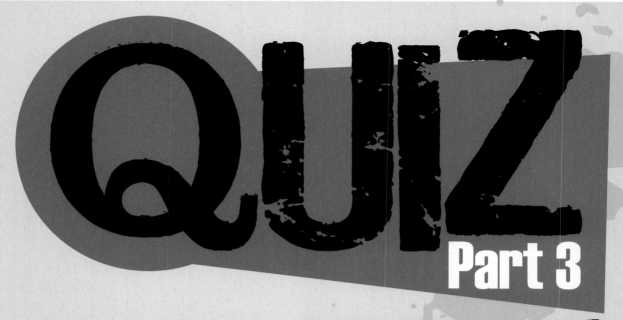

QUIZ
Part 3

THE EARLY YEARS

So how much have you found out about the boys when they were children? Answer the questions below and don't forget to carry your score forward.

Whose first ever performance was at a holiday camp at the age of six?

Where did Jay grow up?

Who has seven brothers and sisters?

Who learned to play guitar with the song 'Wonderwall'?

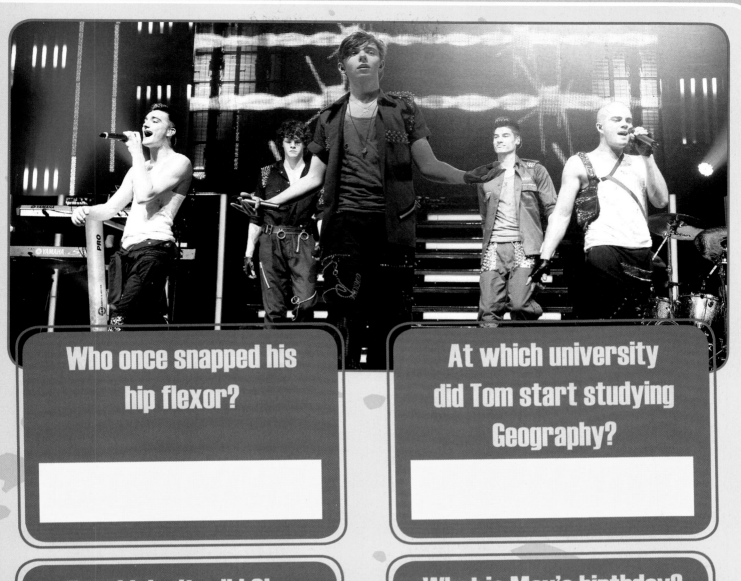

Who once snapped his hip flexor?

At which university did Tom start studying Geography?

To which city did Siva go to pursue his modelling career?

What is Max's birthday?

Which band member is vegetarian?

Where did Nathan go to school?

GETTING TO KNOW...

NATHAN

What's the best thing that's happened to you since forming The Wanted?
Performing at Wembley Stadium for the second time ... I mean, the first time was amazing but the second time we got to do a few more tracks so I could really enjoy the moment instead of concentrating on not going wrong!

What did you like best about school?
Hometime was always good! But I suppose my mates aren't bad either!

What's your idea of the perfect date?
Not messing it up or saying something awkward or inappropriate like I usually do!

How do you cope with the busy life of being in a band?
Not messing it up or saying something awkward or inappropriate like I usually do!.

Do you have any pets?
Yes! I have a cat called Tia, a dog called Harry and a snake called Charlie.

What do you hope your life is like in ten years?
I hope its good!! I want to have written some amazing songs and played some amazing gigs ... a bit of cash wouldn't go amiss either!

What was your favourite TV show when you were young?
Gladiator.

What's your favourite sport?
Football.

What's your favourite thing about yourself?
My unique sense of humour.

What makes you laugh?
Awkward people.

Do you think you would make a good boyfriend?
I would try and make her feel like the best girl in the world ... So I hope that's a yes!

If you weren't in The Wanted, what do you think you would be doing?
I would be trying to find a job as I probably wouldn't of got into university!

Do you prefer singing live or recording in a studio?
Singing live, even though it sometimes doesn't always go to plan!.

What's your earliest memory?
Trying to play the piano when I was around the age of 3!

How would you like to be remembered?
As the guy who entertained, made people smile and sometimes sang good!

Who would like to sing a duet with?
Stevie Wonder.

Are you a city lad or a country boy at heart?
Country boy!!!

Are you a fashion fanatic?
Nah not really, just wear what I like, not what people deem to be fashionable. People should only wear what they feel comfortable in.

Are you allergic to anything?
Smelly people.

What's your most annoying habit?
Making people feel awkward.

Do you have any superstitions?
Don't walk under a ladder, it could fall and hurt you ....

How do you keep fit?
Jump around the stage like an idiot for an hour during a gig!

What's your favourite The Wanted lyric and why?
"Standing here in this burning room" was created from a really strong image of the signs that everything around you had fallen apart. The lyric is from a track we have written for the new album.

Do you believe in love at first sight?
To fall in love at first sight is the same as falling in love with someones appearance, not the person they really are. So in that case ... Yes, I do .... I joke!!!

Do you do your own shopping?
Who doesn't!? Of course I do!

What's your favourite place in the UK?
Gloucester.

What do you do to relax?
Listen to music, chill with mates or play on my ps3.

0061096
NATHAN SYKES
LAS VEGAS POLICE DEPT

THE YAMATTE

Star SECRETS

What does 2012 hold for you and The Wanted?

MAX

Star sign:
Virgo
Element:
Earth
Type:
Mutable – the communicator
Planet:
Mercury
Character words:
analytical, detailed, loyal,
perfectionist, elegant

JAY AND TOM

Star sign:
Leo
Element:
Fire
Type:
Fixed – the boss
Planet:
Sun
Character words:
powerful, confident, loving,
faithful, bold

SIVA

Star sign:
Scorpio
Element:
Water
Type:
Fixed – the boss
Planet:
Pluto
Character words:
creative, possessive, passionate,
self-contained

NATHAN

Star sign:
Aries
Element:
Fire
Type:
Cardinal – the action hero
Planet:
Mars
Character words:
brave, impatient, energetic, leader

Star SECRETS

ARIES
Mar 21 – April 20

Fame: Your place is in the limelight, the centre of attention!
Friends: Your friends will really need you this year. Make sure you are always there for them, because there will come a time when you need them just as much.
Life: This year will be packed with changes for you. Keep a diary to make sure you don't forget a thing.

TAURUS
April 21 – May 21

Fame: You prefer to keep out of the spotlight – you're happy with your life just the way it is!
Friends: Make sure that you spend time with a friend that you haven't seen for a while – she needs you.
Life: You should try something new this year – it'll be a huge success.

GEMINI
May 22 – Jun 21

Fame: Sometimes you love being the centre of attention, but there are times when you need to be alone. If you are seeking fame and fortune, don't forget to make some space for you-time!
Friends: True friends love you for who you are – don't let anyone try to change you.
Life: This year will be full of highs and lows. But don't feel blue – by the end of the year you'll be saying it was the best ever!

CANCER
Jun 22 – Jul 23

Fame: You are equally at home in front of the camera and behind it – just as long as you are part of the action!
Friends: You and your BFF have the best rapport ever – your friendship will just keep getting stronger.
Life: This year you will find that happiness comes easily – and summertime will definitely be the highlight!

LEO
Jan 21 – Feb 19

Fame: Leo, you were born to be famous! Don't be afraid to take your place among the stars.
Friends: Watch out for false friends who make promises they can't keep. Stay loyal to your BFFs – they'll always be there for you.
Life: School can seem like a drag, but if you keep your head down this year, there will some awesome rewards ahead!

VIRGO
Feb 20 – Mar 20

Fame: You will succeed at anything you put your mind to, so focus on your ambition and go for it!
Friends: Trust in yourself a bit more, because you are a great friend.
Life: 2012 is going to be your year. Make sure you take time to have a holiday – it'll turn out to be a real high point for you!

Mar 21 – April 20

LIBRA

Fame: You have the potential to be a truly unforgettable star, so be brave and seize the day!

Friends: This year is going to be full of new friends and fantastic experiences – enjoy!

Life: Adventures wait around every corner – just relax and have some fun, because you deserve it.

April 21 – May 21

SCORPIO

Fame: Stardom isn't the most important thing for you – it's people who really count. Focus on caring for the people you love.

Friends: Learn to trust other people a little more – they only have your best interests at heart.

Life: Your determination will carry you towards your ultimate goals this year – good luck is shining on you!

May 22 – Jun 21

SAGITTARIUS

Fame: Hard work will make your dreams come true.

Friends: Don't take your friends for granted just because you're busy.

Life: There are tons of opportunities heading your way, but take the time to look before you leap!

Jun 22 – Jul 23

CAPRICORN

Fame: You may not end up on the cover of a magazine, but you have a magical quality that will make sure everyone notices you.

Friends: Try to notice how your friends are feeling a little more. Sometimes your enthusiasm carries you away and you forget to listen.

Life: You are going to love 2012! It will be full of fun and good times.

Jan 21 – Feb 19

AQUARIUS

Fame: You love meeting new people and trying new things, so you would love living in the spotlight. Expect the unexpected!

Friends: Friends won't always do the right thing, but their hearts are in the right place. Practise a little patience and it'll be a great year for you.

Life: You don't need to worry – this year is going to totally rock!

Feb 20 – Mar 20

PISCES

Fame: Your reserved nature means that you're not a fame-seeker. However, you are super-creative, so perhaps song-writing is where your talents will take you.

Friends: It's important to let your friends know how much they mean to you. Organise a party just for them!

Life: There are so many amazing things heading your way! Learn to look forward to the next bend in the road.

Stars 2012

QUIZ
Part 4

GETTING TOGETHER

How did it all start? Have you been a fan right from the beginning?
See how many facts you know about the birth of The Wanted.

How long did the audition process take?

Who sang one of his own songs at the audition?

How long did the boot camp process last?

Siva's brother also auditioned for the band – but what is his name?

One of Max's dogs is named after which American singing superstar?

Where did the boys start their schools tour?

Which people were banned from the tour bus?

What is Max's favourite TV show?

Which countries are the boys of The Wanted from?

In which year did The Wanted form?

MUSIC MAD

The Wanted are passionate about music, and they love creating unforgettable lyrics. Have you ever written a song? Get started by thinking up some song titles...

1. --
2. --
3. --
4. --
5. --

Now you really need to crank up your imagination! Did you know that poems are just songs without a tune? Try writing a poem about someone you love. It could be a friend, a pet, a member of your family or even The Wanted! Below are some semi-rhyming words to inspire you – how many will end up in your poem?

LOVE – ABOVE – ENOUGH
HEART – START – APART – DART – ART
FUN – SUN – DONE – RUN – BEGUN
GIRL – WHIRL – CURL – TWIRL
BOY – ANNOY – JOY – TOY
SWEET – STREET – NEAT – FEET
DAZED – AMAZED – CRAZED
LIFE – WIFE – KNIFE – RIFE
EYES – SPIES – TRIES – CRIES – LIES – HIGHS
TRUE – WHO – YOU – NEW – FLEW
BIRD – HEARD – WORD – ABSURD

Finally you need a catchy tune to hook the listeners! Say your poem aloud and feel the rhythm of the words. Then try to come up with the perfect melody!

My Poem:

GLAD YOU CAME

The WANTED

GLAD YOU CAME

The ___ goes down the ___ come out
And all that ___ is here and ___
My ___ will never be the same I'm glad you came

You cast a ___ on me, ___ on me
You ___ me like the ___ fell on me, fell on me
And I decided you ___ well on me, well on me
So lets go ___ no one else can see ___ and ___

Turn the ___ out now
Now I'll ___ you by the ___
Hand you another ___, ___ it if you can,
Can you spend a little time
___ is slipping away
Away from us so ___
Stay with ___ I can make make you glad you came

The ___ goes down the ___ come out
And all that ___ is here and now
My ___ will never be the same I'm glad you came

You cast a spell on me, spell on me
You ___ me like the ___ fell on me, fell on me
And I ___ you look well on me, well on me
So lets go ___ no one else can see you and me

Turn the ___ out now
Now I'll take you by the ___
Hand you another ___, ___ it if you can
Can you ___ a little time
Time is slipping away
___ from us so stay
___ with me I can make, make you glad you came

The ___ goes down the ___ come out
And all that ___ is here and now
My ___ will never be the same I'm glad you came
I'm glad you came
___ so glad you came
I'm glad you came
I'm glad you came

The ___ goes down the ___ come out
And all that counts is here and now
My ___ will never be the same I'm glad you ___

TOUR GUIDE 2012

February 2012

15 - **Nottingham Capital FM Arena**
17 - **Manchester MEN Arena**
18 - **Sheffield Motorpoint Arena**
20 - **Brighton Centre**
23 - **Cardiff Arena**
24 - **Liverpool Echo Arena**
25 - **Newcastle Metro Arena**
27 - **Glasgow SECC**
28 - **Aberdeen AECC**

March 2012

01 - **Birmingham LG Arena**
02 - **Bournemouth BIC**
03 - **London 02 Arena**
05 - **Brighton Centre**
06 - **Bournemouth BIC**
08 - **Belfast Odyssey Arena**
09 - **Dublin 02 Arena**

QUIZ Part 5

STAR SOUNDBITES

You might know all about what they sing, but how closely do you pay attention to the things that The Wanted say? See if you can remember who said these one-liners!

"I'm officially legal!"

"We're just average lads, from working-class backgrounds."

"To be even mentioned in the same breath as JLS is a compliment."

"I was the odd one out, the rubbish kid who didn't like football!"

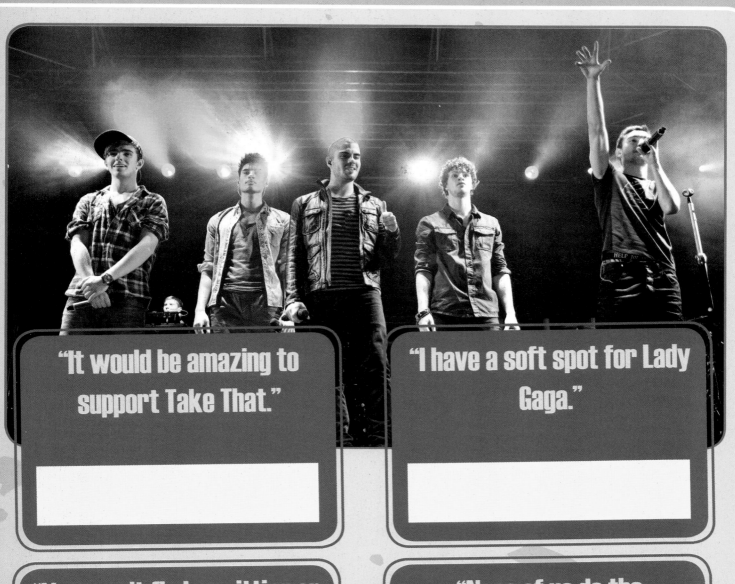

"It would be amazing to support Take That."

"I have a soft spot for Lady Gaga."

"You won't find us sitting on stools in our suits and standing up for the key change!"

"None of us do the washing-up!"

"I have nothing but brilliant memories of The X Factor."

"I'm a bit of an old man really. I just sit in the corner with a nice cup of tea!"

The WANTED

The WANTED
SCRAP BOOK

A day at the races
Hanging out at
Newbury Racecourse.

Place your bets please!
Did we win?

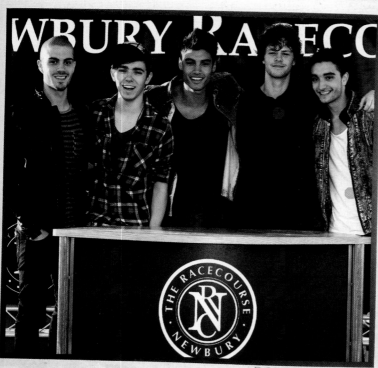

Say cheese!
There's just time for one last
photo before the live show . . .

Playing live
We had so much fun on stage at Newbury!

Wave your hands in the air . . .
The audience was fantastic!

Up where we belong
You can't beat the buzz of performing live.

89

The WANTED
SCRAP BOOK

CIA Cardiff
Cardiff is a wicked venue – can't wait to perform there again.

Guitar man
How cool is our job?!

Siva Fever
The girls screamed their heads off for Siva!

Keeping it real
We love the chance to play our instruments so we included an acoustic set.

Loving the audience participation
We had the whole arena singing along with us.

A dream gig
Singing to an arena packed full of our fans is the best feeling in the world!

ANSWERS

Quiz 1 - Pages 22-23
Tom.
'All Time Low'.
Avenue.
Geffen.
'Gold Forever'.
Yes.
Max.
Siva and Jay.
Gloucester.
Tom.

Quiz 2 - Page 40-42
'Seen the change watching it fade.'
'When I'm standing on the yellow line.'
'Fill my head with white noise.'
'You get bored and I get cold feet.'
'If we don't take it on we won't get far.'
'I feel your heart cry for love.'
'Hope you can't see the creases and they've ordered the pizzas.'
'Now this melody's a healer.'
'Just two kids stupid and fearless.'
'Cry your tears on my shoulder.'

Page 56-57
Nathan
Newark, Nottinghamshire.
Siva
Tom
Max
Manchester Met University.
London
6th September 1988
Jay
The Sylvia Young Theatre School.

Quiz 4 - Page 76-78
Nine months.
Tom
Four days.
Kumar.
Elvis
Girls.
The X Factor.
England and Ireland.
2009

Quiz 5 - Page 84-85
Nathan
Max
Siva
Jay
Jay
Max
Nathan
Tom
Max
Nathan

Page 44 Wordsearch

N	S	D	N	E	I	R	F	A	N	S
I	N	R	S	G	E	A	V	F	S	O
S	O	G	A	A	A	I	S	W	N	N
D	I	D	U	T	S	C	E	M	A	F
G	T	N	T	S	I	M	M	S	T	S
A	I	V	G	R	B	U	R	E	H	E
J	D	N	Y	L	S	B	G	C	A	C
J	U	L	S	I	E	L	T	T	N	M
J	A	Y	C	W	S	A	T	O	U	R
J	R	E	S	M	A	X	T	A	M	Y
W	E	M	B	L	E	Y	N	J	I	B

Page 45 Crossword

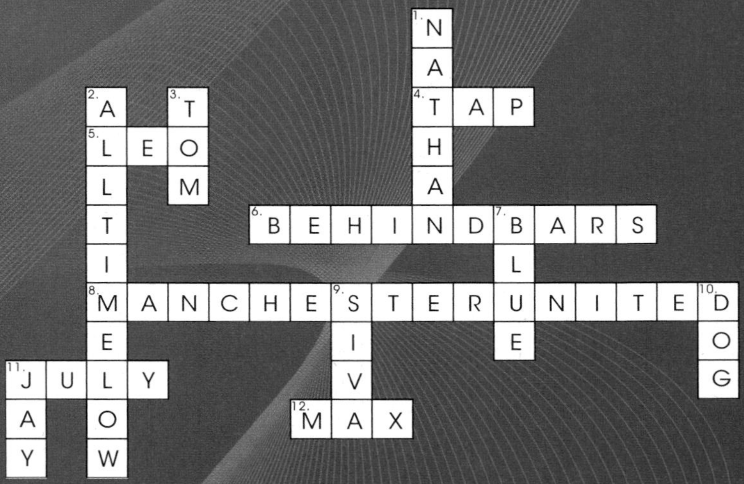

1. NATHAN
2. ALLTIMELOW
3. TOM
4. TAP
5. LEO
6. BEHINDBARS
7. BALLIE
8. MANCHESTERUNITED
9. SIVA
10. DOG
11. JULY
12. MAX
JAY